FACT FINDERS

Educational Adviser : Arthur Razzell

Early Man

Anthony Harvey and Judith Diment

Illustrated by Angus McBride
Designed by Faulkner/Marks Partnership

Macmillan Education Limited

© 1976 Macmillan Education Limited
Published in the United
States by Silver Burdett
Company, Morristown, N.J.
1981 Printing
ISBN 0-382-06621-9
Library of Congress
Catalog Card No. 81-83999

Early Man

Different Kinds of Men

There have been several different kinds of Man. The oldest kind probably lived five million years ago. Over the years man has changed.

Peking

Australopithecine

Neanderthal

He has lost much of the hair that once covered his body. His brain has increased in size. The shape of his face has changed. He has become taller.

Cro-Magnon

What is Man?

Man belongs to a group of animals called primates. Apes, monkeys and chimpanzees are also primates. Primates can grasp things with their fingers. Their eyes look to the front, not to the side like a cat's.

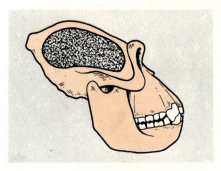

Brain of chimpanzee

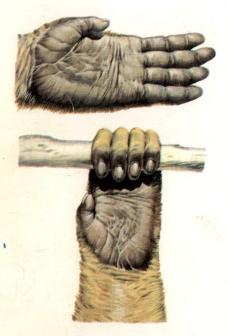

A chimpanzee can grasp a branch with its hand.

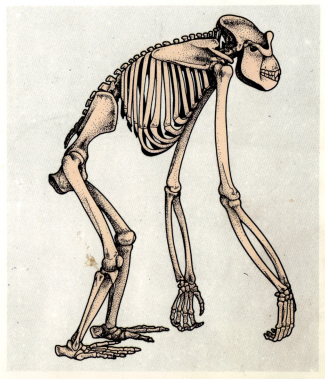

Chimpanzee skeleton

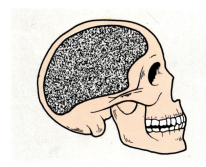

Brain of human

Primates have nails on their fingers and toes, where many other animals have claws. Man is different from the apes, however. His skull and teeth are different. He can put his foot flat on the ground. His brain is larger than other primates.

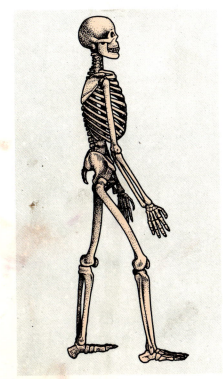

Human skeleton

Man can use his hands to strike fire from flint.

The First Men

The earliest men are called
australopithecines (Southern Apes).
They were about 1.4 metres tall, and
stooped as they walked. They lived
in small groups.

The Coming of Fire

Homo erectus (erect man) was larger than the Southern Apes. He had a bigger brain. These people learned to use fire for warmth, and to cook food. They also used fire for protection against wild animals.

The Cave Men

Neanderthal man is the cave man of stories. He killed animals, such as cave bears, by forcing them over cliffs or into pits. He lived in caves or tents.

The First Modern Men

Cro-Magnon man lived at the end of the Old Stone Age. They used spears and bows and arrows. They also used needles to make clothes from animal skins. They lived in rock shelters.

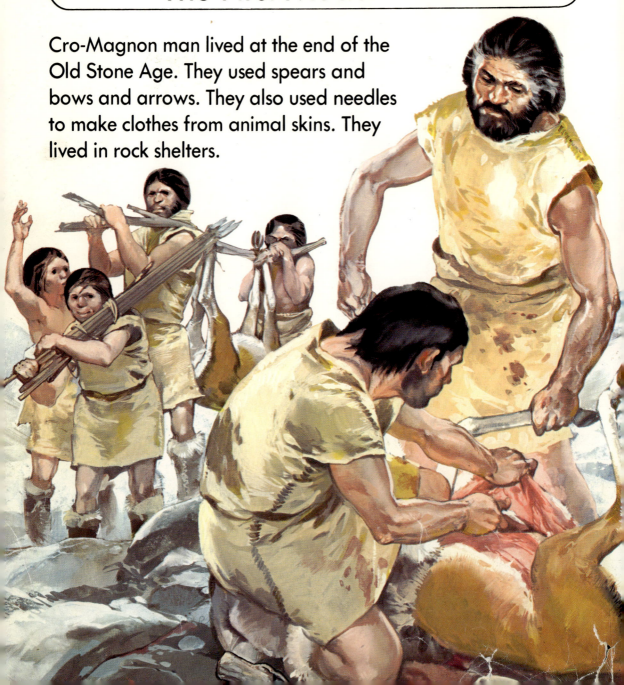

Cave Paintings

The oldest paintings in the world are over twenty thousand years old. They appear on the walls of caves.

Some of the best-known cave paintings are on the walls of a cave in Lascaux, France (below).

The little sculpture was found in Norfolk, England.

Cave painting
by Bushmen,
Southern Africa.

The First Farmers

Neolithic men had permanent homes and lived in villages.
They were the first farmers, and grew wheat and barley.
They tamed animals, and spun cotton and wool to
make clothes.

These people hunted with bows and arrows, and fished with nets.

From Stone to Metal

Until the end of Neolithic times, people made tools from flint or other stones. They dug mines to get the best flint. Remains of these mines have been found in parts of Europe.

Flint axe

Copper axe head

Later, men learned how to make tools and weapons from metal. The first metal used was copper. Then tin was discovered. Bronze is a mixture of tin and copper. The new period was called the Bronze Age.

Glossary

Australopithecine Earliest member of the family of Man.

Bronze Age A period when man made tools of bronze.

Cave Bear A giant bear, about three metres tall.

Cave Paintings Paintings by early Man, mainly of animals, on the walls of caves.

Cro-Magnon A race of people that look like modern Man. They lived in the most recent part of the Old Stone Age.

Homo erectus Name given to the first real men, such as Java man and Peking man.

Mammals Warm blooded animals who feed their young with milk, and have hair or fur.

Man A primate with a very well developed brain.

Neanderthal Man A group of people living in Europe and the Middle East from 100,000 to 35,000 years ago.

Neolithic The time when farming began. It is sometimes called the New Stone Age.

Primates Animals, such as Man and the apes, which can grasp objects with their fingers.

Stone Age A time when Man made his tools of stone. It is divided into the Old, Middle and New Stone Ages.

1 2 3 4 5 6 7 8 9 10— R —85 84 83 82 81